CONCERTO for EUPHONIUM and Concert Band*

Robert Jager

Euphonium and Piano Reduction

In 3 Movements

I. Slowly, dramatically, freely   ca. 4:02

II. Slowly, reflectively   ca. 4:28

III. Brightly, but forcefully   ca. 3:28

Total Duration   ca. 12 minutes

*Concert Band or Symphony Orchestra
Accompaniments on rental

EXCLUSIVELY DISTRIBUTED BY

HAL•LEONARD® CORPORATION

7777 W. BLUEMOUND RD. P.O. BOX 13819 MILWAUKEE, WI 53213

CONCERTO for EUPHONIUM
Robert Jager

PROGRAM NOTE

Robert Jager's CONCERTO FOR EUPHONIUM was originally commissioned by the Phi Mu Alpha Sinfonia chapter at the Cincinnati College Conservatory of Music as a concerto for trombone and orchestra. In 1996, Jager decided to rewrite and rescore the work as a concerto for euphonium with accompaniments for band, orchestra and piano. The trombone version no longer exists.

The CONCERTO FOR EUPHONIUM is a highly demanding work for both the soloist and the accompaniment. The outer movements are filled with rhythmic and metric complexities that demand a virtuoso group of musicians. The second movement, while less technically demanding, requires mature musicians because of its sensitive lines and shaded instrumental colors.

After a dramatic introduction dominated by the euphonium, wherein all of the principal motives of the work are stated, the music in the first movement moves into a highly rhythmic dialogue between the soloist and the ensemble. Numerous solos in the ensemble echo the material first stated by the euphonium. After a good deal of "give and take," the movement ends quietly preparing for the next movement.

The second movement is designated to be played "slowly and reflectively." It is this mood, one of reflection, that dominates the quasi-impressionistic character of the music. Instrumental color from the ensemble is highlighted as the long, lyrical lines of the soloist unfold.

The third movement returns to the fiery, rhythmic character of the first movement, but this time more emphasis is placed upon mixed and asymmetrical meters, so that the solid feel of the barline is lost. Like the first movement, there is much dialogue between the euphonium and the ensemble soloists. The form of this movement is that of a "rondo," and in the typical capricious mood of the rondo literally rushes headlong into an exciting and brilliant finale.

THE COMPOSER

Robert Jager, a native of Birmingham, New York, graduated from the University of Michigan and spent four years (1962-1966) as staff arranger/composer for the Armed Forces School of Music. Presently, he is Professor of Music and coordinator of academic studies in music at the Tennessee Technological University in Cookville, TN.

Widely commissioned and performed, Jager has works published for band, orchestra and chamber groups. His awards in music include the American Bandmasters Association's Ostwald Award (its only three-time recipient), the Kappa Kappa Psi's Distinguished Service Medal for composition, NSOA's Roth Award, NBA's Citation of Excellence and various academic honors.

His composition "The Wall," dedicated to the men and women lost in the Vietnam War, has secured a most unusual acceptance in our nation's Capitol. Commissioned and premiered there by the United States Air Force Band, it soon thereafter had its orchestral premiere on the west lawn of the Capitol by the National Symphony Orchestra, with 65,000 persons in attendance.

Jager has appeared often as a conductor and lecturer throughout the United States as well as Canada, Europe and Japan, making a number of record albums in that country.

Concerto for Euphonium

I.

Total Duration: *ca.* 12 minutes

Slowly, dramatically, freely ♩ = *ca.* 58

ROBERT JAGER (1997)

Concerto for Euphonium

II.

Slowly, reflectively ♩ = *ca.* **48**

A little faster ♩ = *ca.* **52**

CONCERTO for EUPHONIUM and Concert Band*

Robert Jager

Euphonium and Piano Reduction

*Concert Band or Symphony Orchestra
Accompaniments on rental

EXCLUSIVELY DISTRIBUTED BY

7777 W. BLUEMOUND RD. P.O. BOX 13819 MILWAUKEE, WI 53213

CONCERTO for EUPHONIUM and Concert Band*

Robert Jager

Euphonium and Piano Reduction

In 3 Movements

I. Slowly, dramatically, freely   ca. 4:02

II. Slowly, reflectively   ca. 4:28

III. Brightly, but forcefully   ca. 3:28

Total Duration   ca. 12 minutes

*Concert Band or Symphony Orchestra
Accompaniments on rental

EDWARD B.
Marks Music
Company

EXCLUSIVELY DISTRIBUTED BY

HAL•LEONARD®
CORPORATION

7777 W. BLUEMOUND RD. P.O. BOX 13819 MILWAUKEE, WI 53213

CONCERTO for EUPHONIUM
Robert Jager

PROGRAM NOTE

Robert Jager's CONCERTO FOR EUPHONIUM was originally commissioned by the Phi Mu Alpha Sinfonia chapter at the Cincinnati College Conservatory of Music as a concerto for trombone and orchestra. In 1996, Jager decided to rewrite and rescore the work as a concerto for euphonium with accompaniments for band, orchestra and piano. The trombone version no longer exists.

The CONCERTO FOR EUPHONIUM is a highly demanding work for both the soloist and the accompaniment. The outer movements are filled with rhythmic and metric complexities that demand a virtuoso group of musicians. The second movement, while less technically demanding, requires mature musicians because of its sensitive lines and shaded instrumental colors.

After a dramatic introduction dominated by the euphonium, wherein all of the principal motives of the work are stated, the music in the first movement moves into a highly rhythmic dialogue between the soloist and the ensemble. Numerous solos in the ensemble echo the material first stated by the euphonium. After a good deal of "give and take," the movement ends quietly preparing for the next movement.

The second movement is designated to be played "slowly and reflectively." It is this mood, one of reflection, that dominates the quasi-impressionistic character of the music. Instrumental color from the ensemble is highlighted as the long, lyrical lines of the soloist unfold.

The third movement returns to the fiery, rhythmic character of the first movement, but this time more emphasis is placed upon mixed and asymmetrical meters, so that the solid feel of the barline is lost. Like the first movement, there is much dialogue between the euphonium and the ensemble soloists. The form of this movement is that of a "rondo," and in the typical capricious mood of the rondo literally rushes headlong into an exciting and brilliant finale.

THE COMPOSER

Robert Jager, a native of Birmingham, New York, graduated from the University of Michigan and spent four years (1962-1966) as staff arranger/composer for the Armed Forces School of Music. Presently, he is Professor of Music and coordinator of academic studies in music at the Tennessee Technological University in Cookville, TN.

Widely commissioned and performed, Jager has works published for band, orchestra and chamber groups. His awards in music include the American Bandmasters Association's Ostwald Award (its only three-time recipient), the Kappa Kappa Psi's Distinguished Service Medal for composition, NSOA's Roth Award, NBA's Citation of Excellence and various academic honors.

His composition "The Wall," dedicated to the men and women lost in the Vietnam War, has secured a most unusual acceptance in our nation's Capitol. Commissioned and premiered there by the United States Air Force Band, it soon thereafter had its orchestral premiere on the west lawn of the Capitol by the National Symphony Orchestra, with 65,000 persons in attendance.

Jager has appeared often as a conductor and lecturer throughout the United States as well as Canada, Europe and Japan, making a number of record albums in that country.

Concerto for Euphonium

I.

SOLO EUPHONIUM

ROBERT JAGER (1997)

II.

Slowly, reflectively ♩ = *ca.* **48**

A little faster ♩ = *ca.* **52**

III.

Brightly, but forcefully ♩ = *ca.* **140**

(Time)

III.

Brightly, but forcefully ♩ = *ca.* **140**

Concerto for Euphonium